Peggy Louise Parrish
Parma, Idaho
All artwork of the interior and cover are by
Peggy Louise Parrish

ISBN-13;978 1542948746
ISBN-10;1542948746

Welcome to an Adventure with Noble N Letters

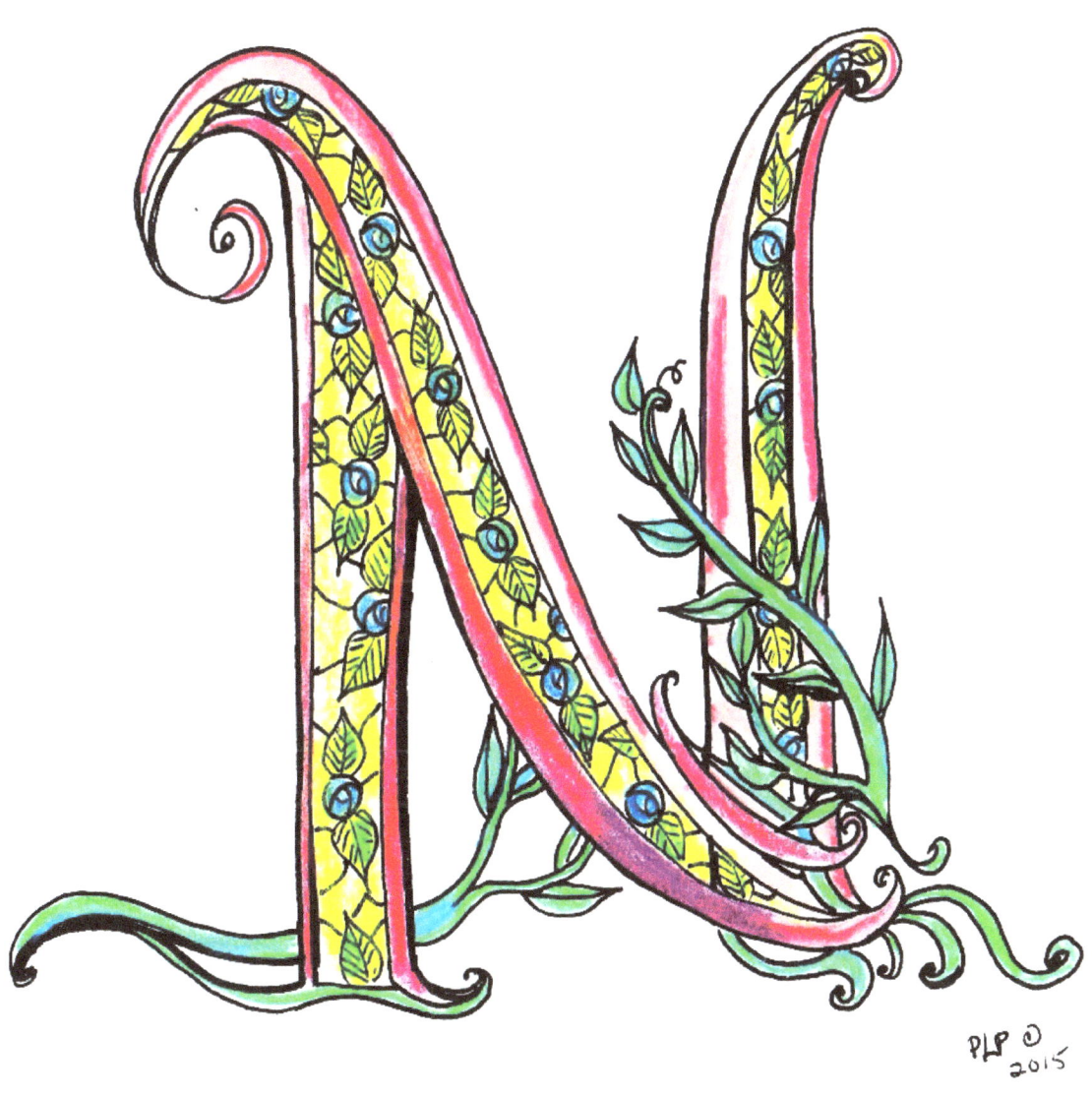

The Noble Letter N

Coloring Book

By Peggy Louise Parrish

C. 2017

Welcome to the Noble Letter N. Artist Peggy Louise Parrish has made this book for others to enjoy coloring her Letter N designs. The preferred medium is usually a quality colored pencil. If watercolor pencils, markers, or paints are used please remember to place a scrap paper behind the page you are completing.

Perhaps your first or last name starts with a letter N. Go ahead and enjoy choosing whatever colors you want. Leave the artist initials on the bottom of each page. Why not put colored by and your own name on the letters you are satisfied with. Hopefully you will be spurred on to do even more art and more exploration with Letter N after this book.

Get Ready, Get started...Now Go Color.....

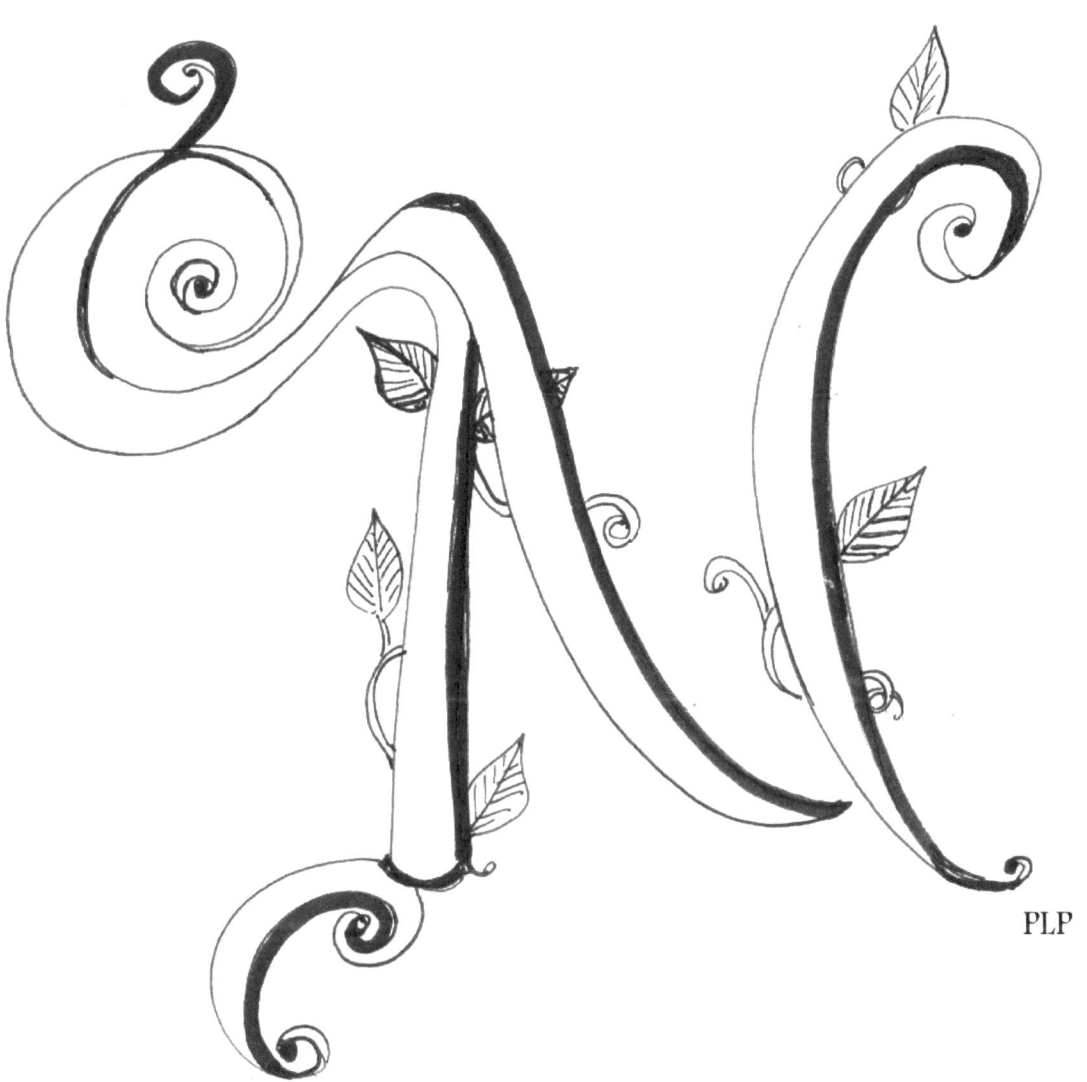

PLP

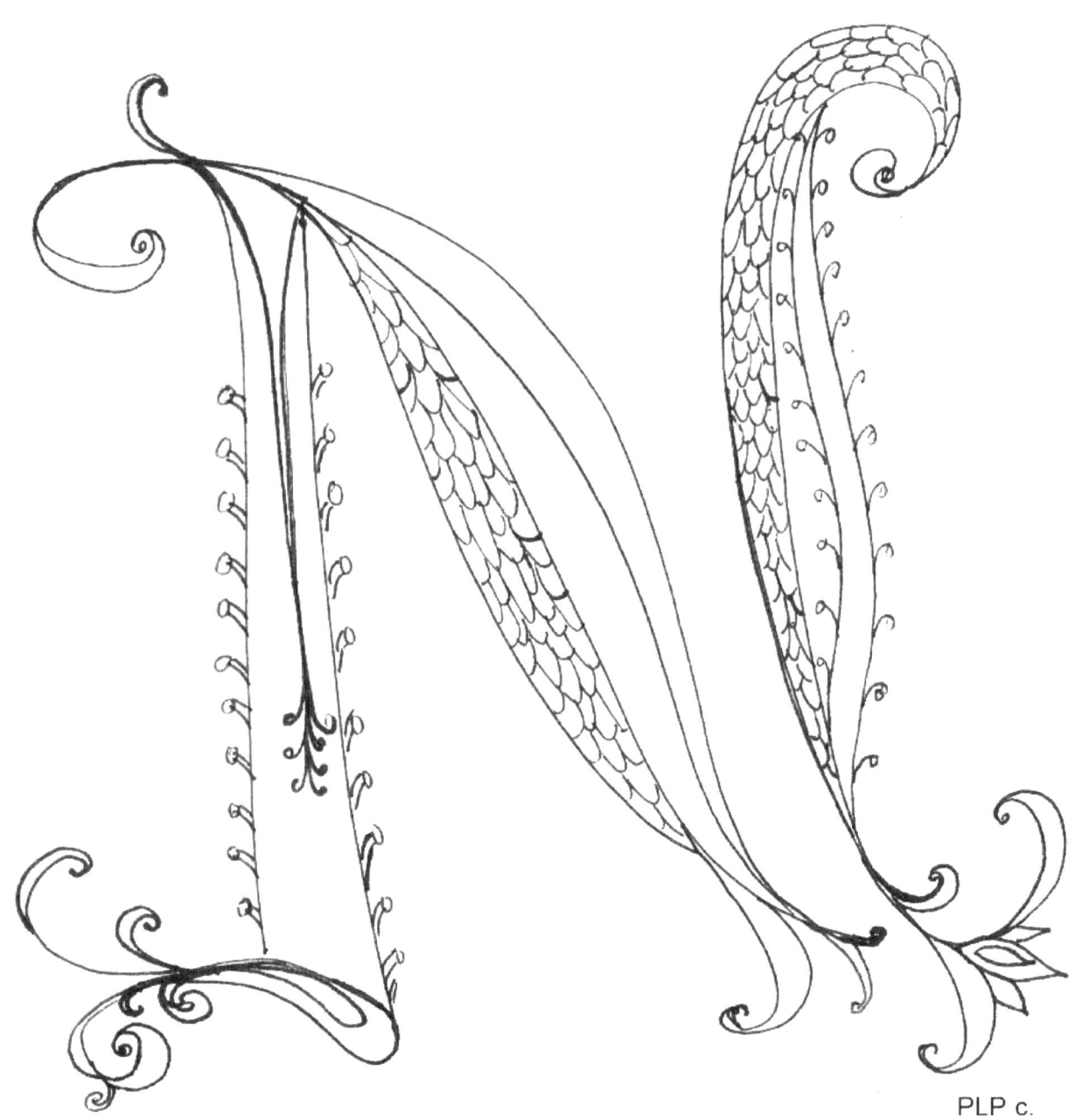

PLP c.

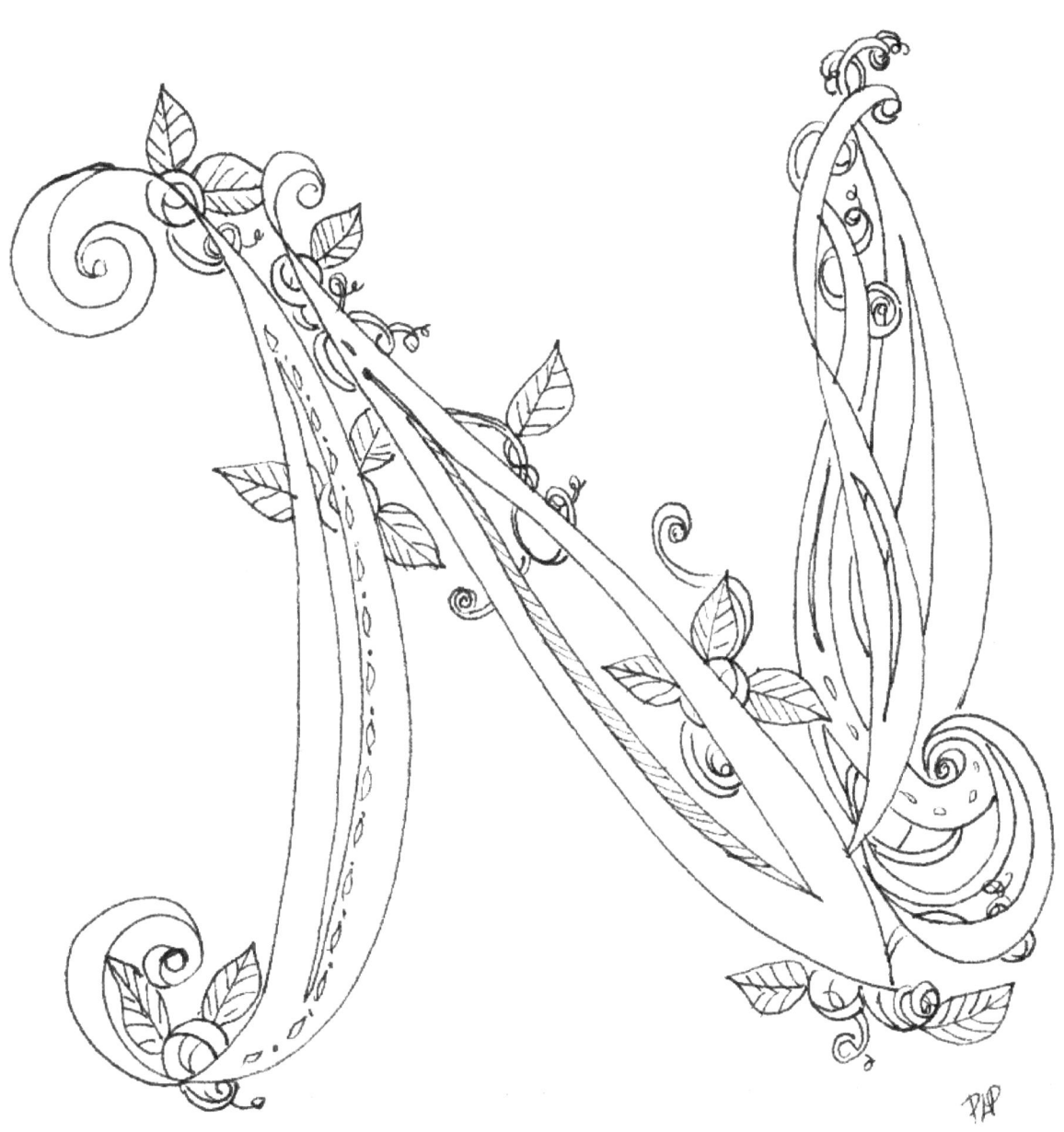

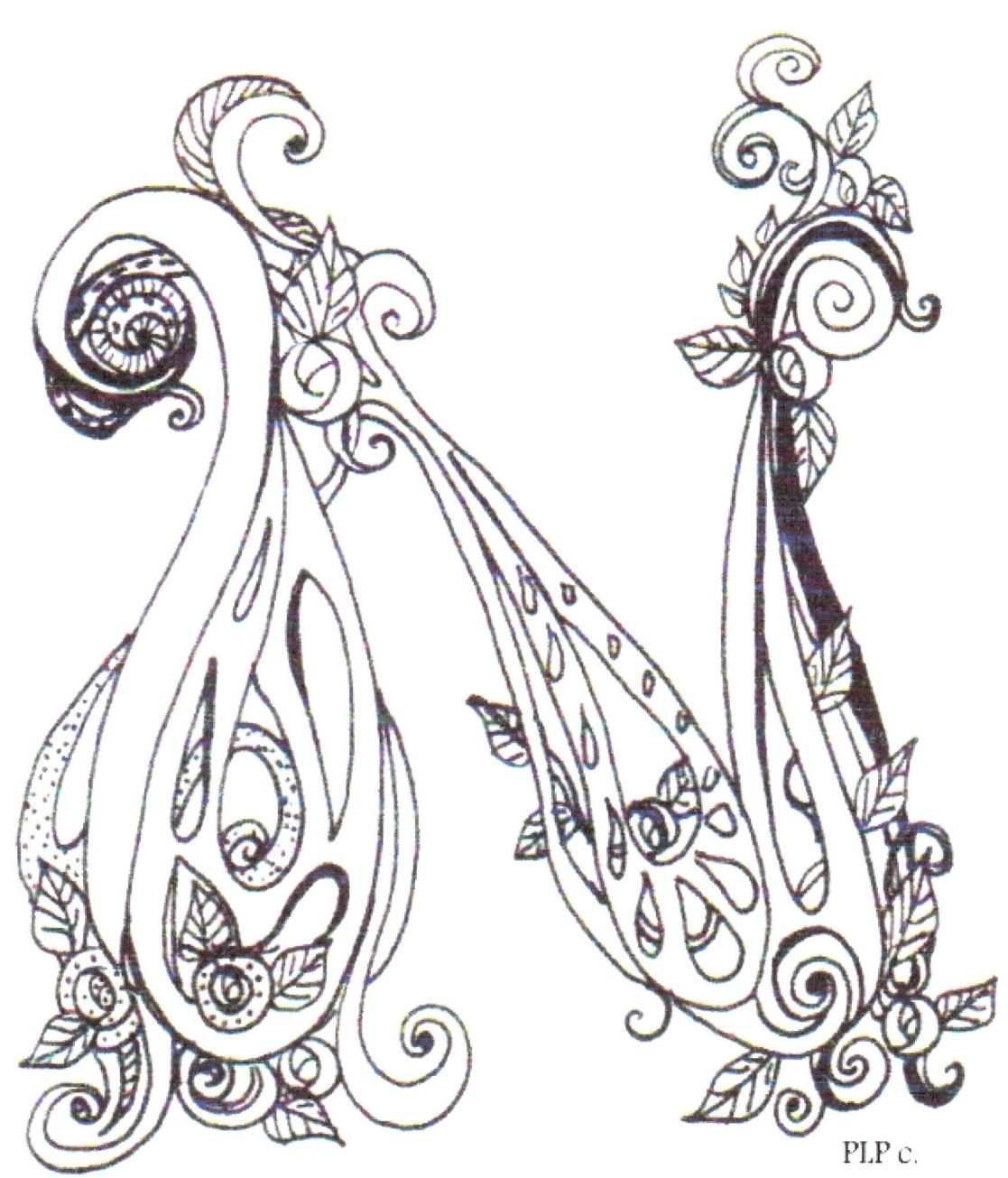

PLP c.

PLP C.

PLP c.

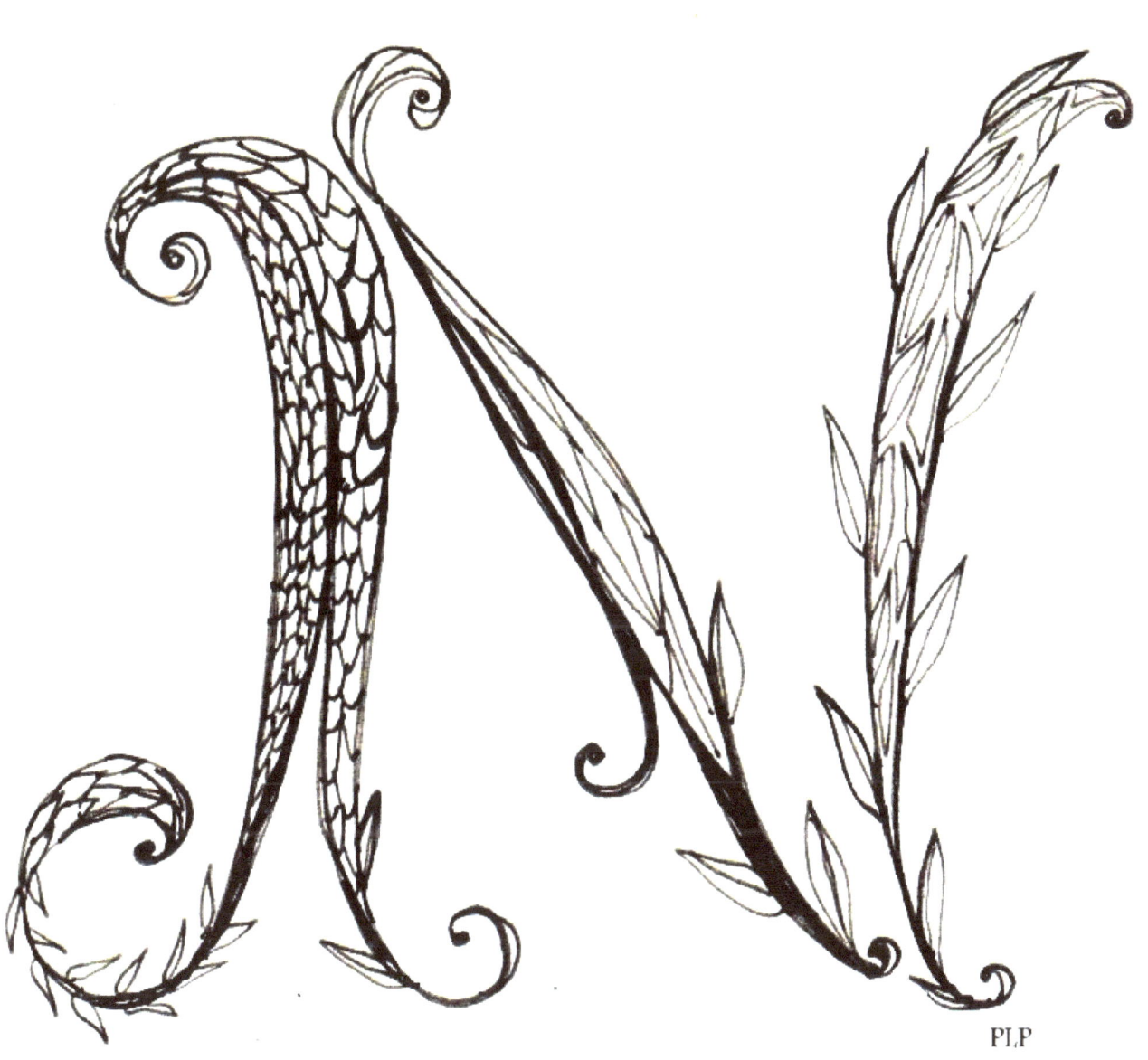

PLP

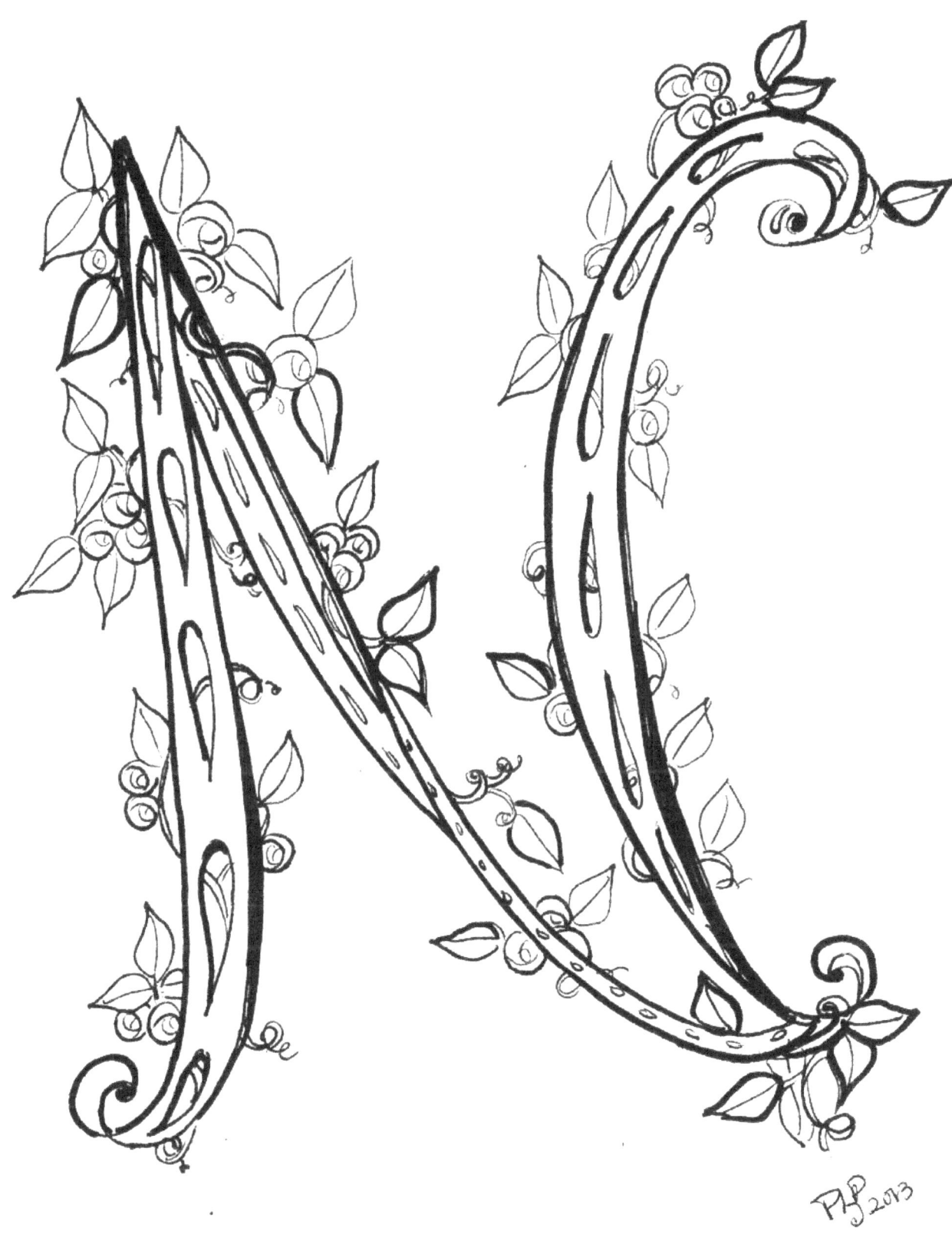

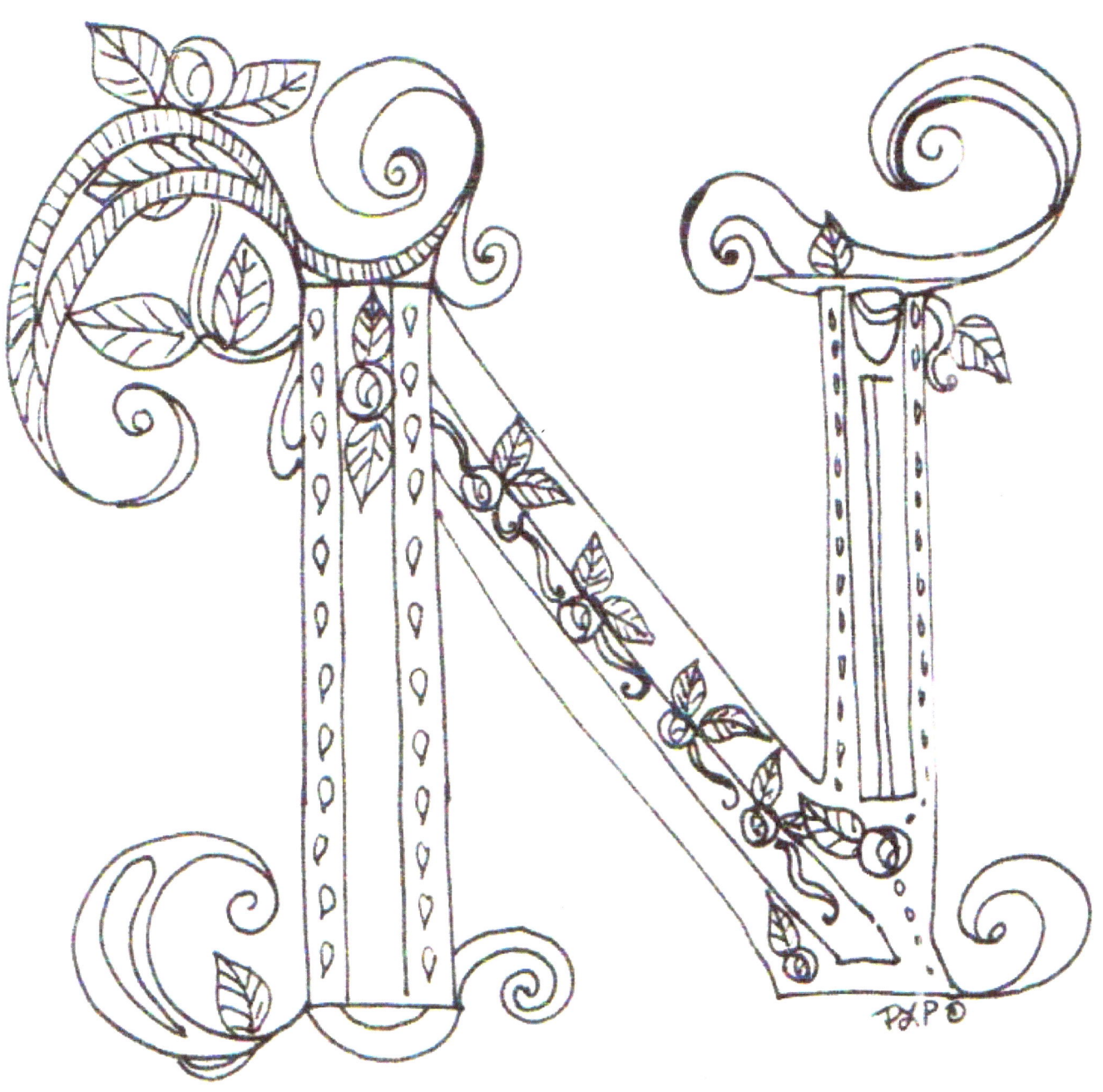

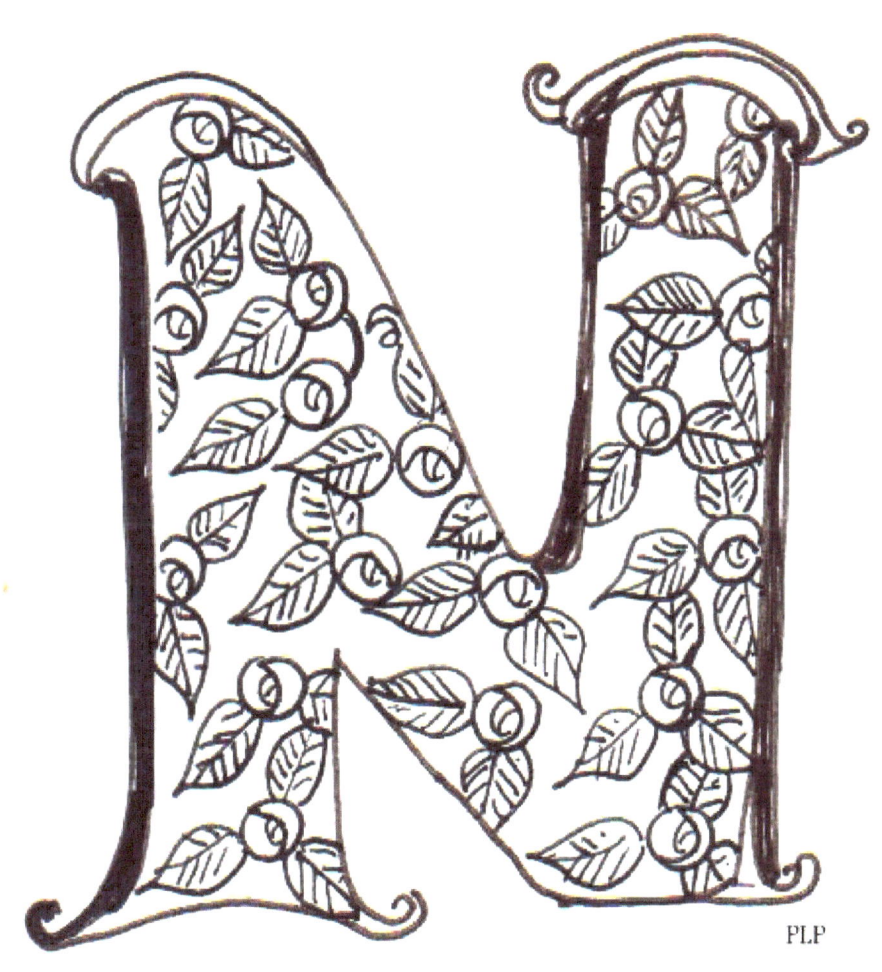

PLP

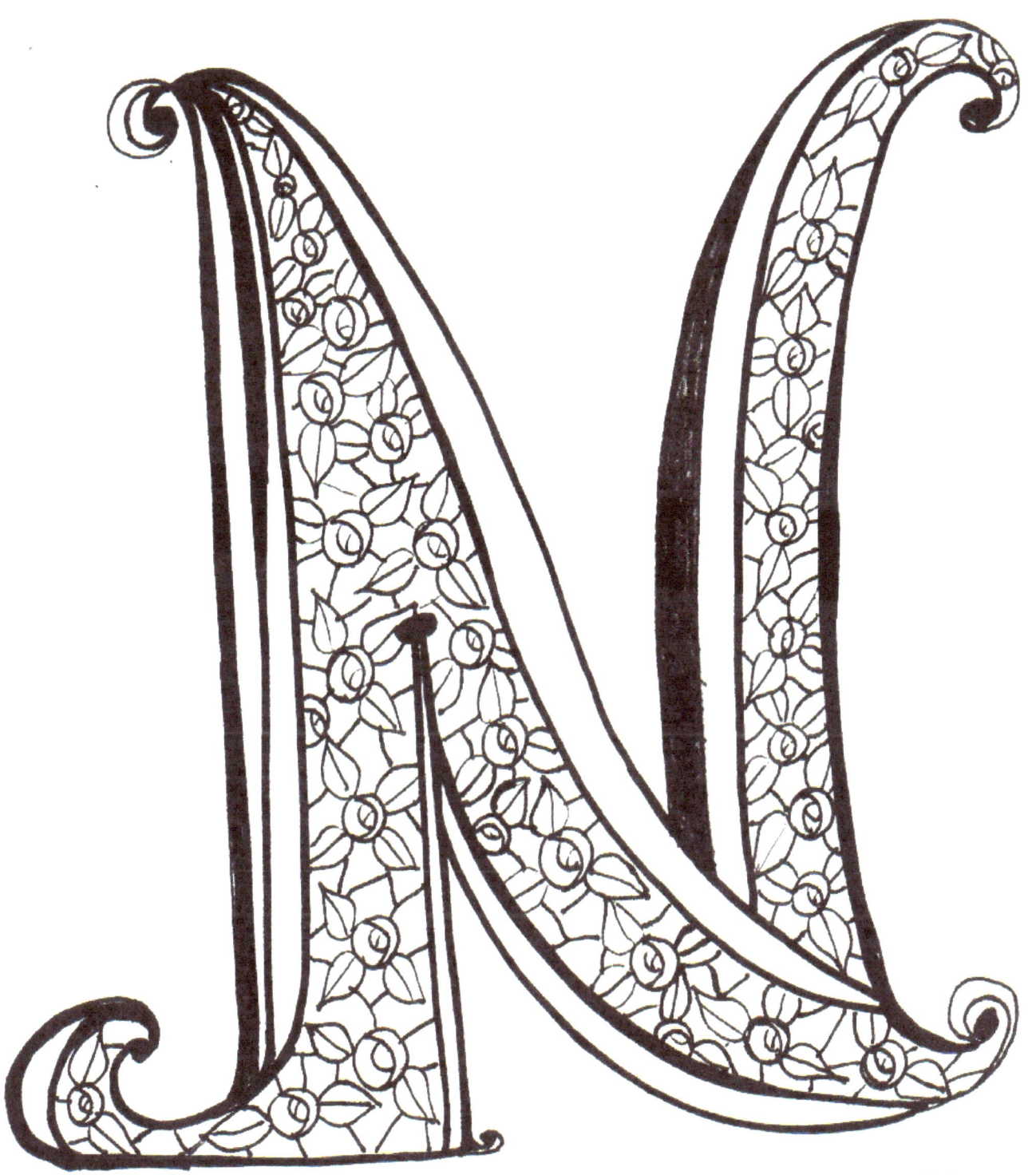

PLP c.

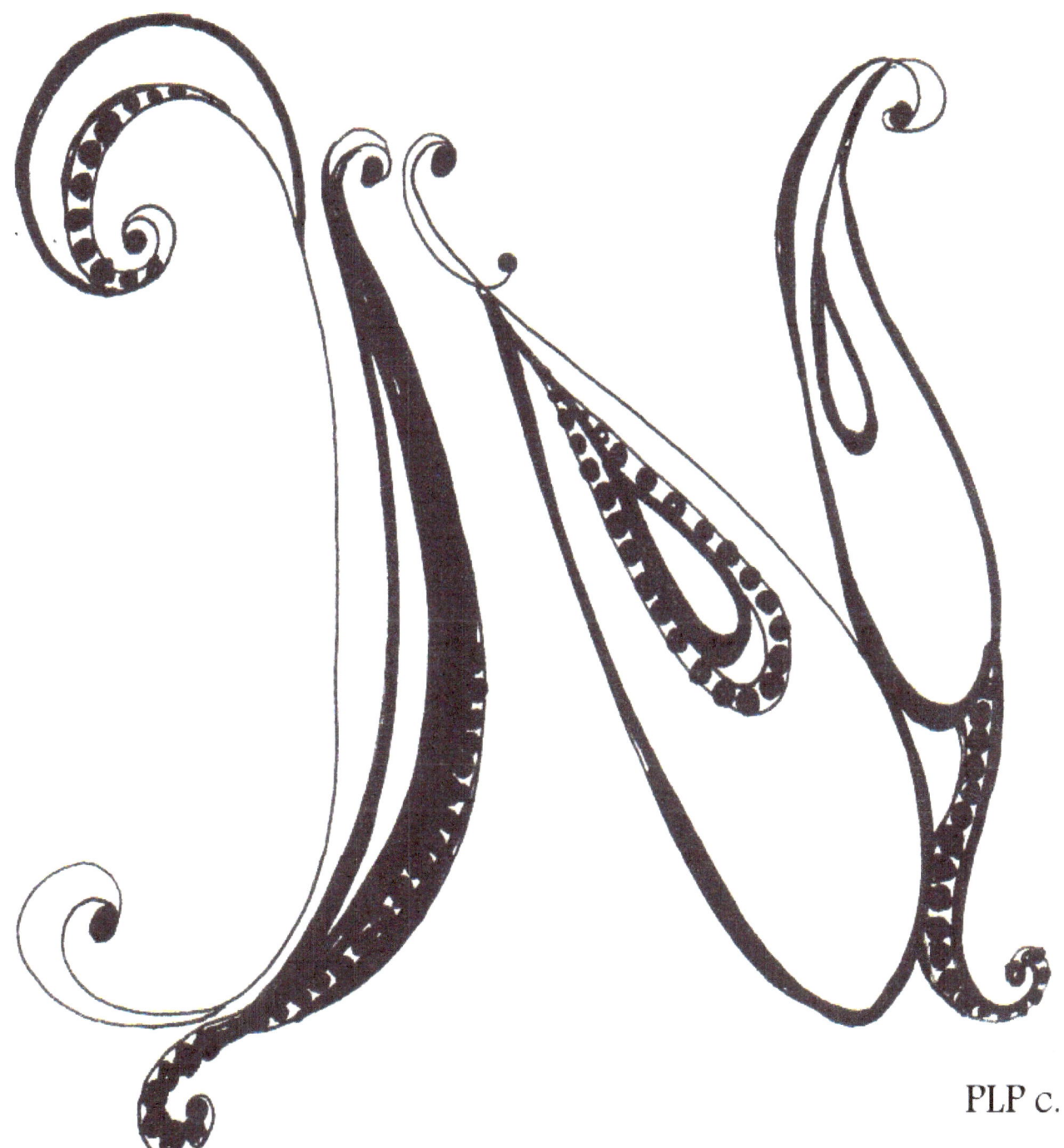

PLP c.

PLP
©2013

A Wallpaper is fun to surround your letter with.

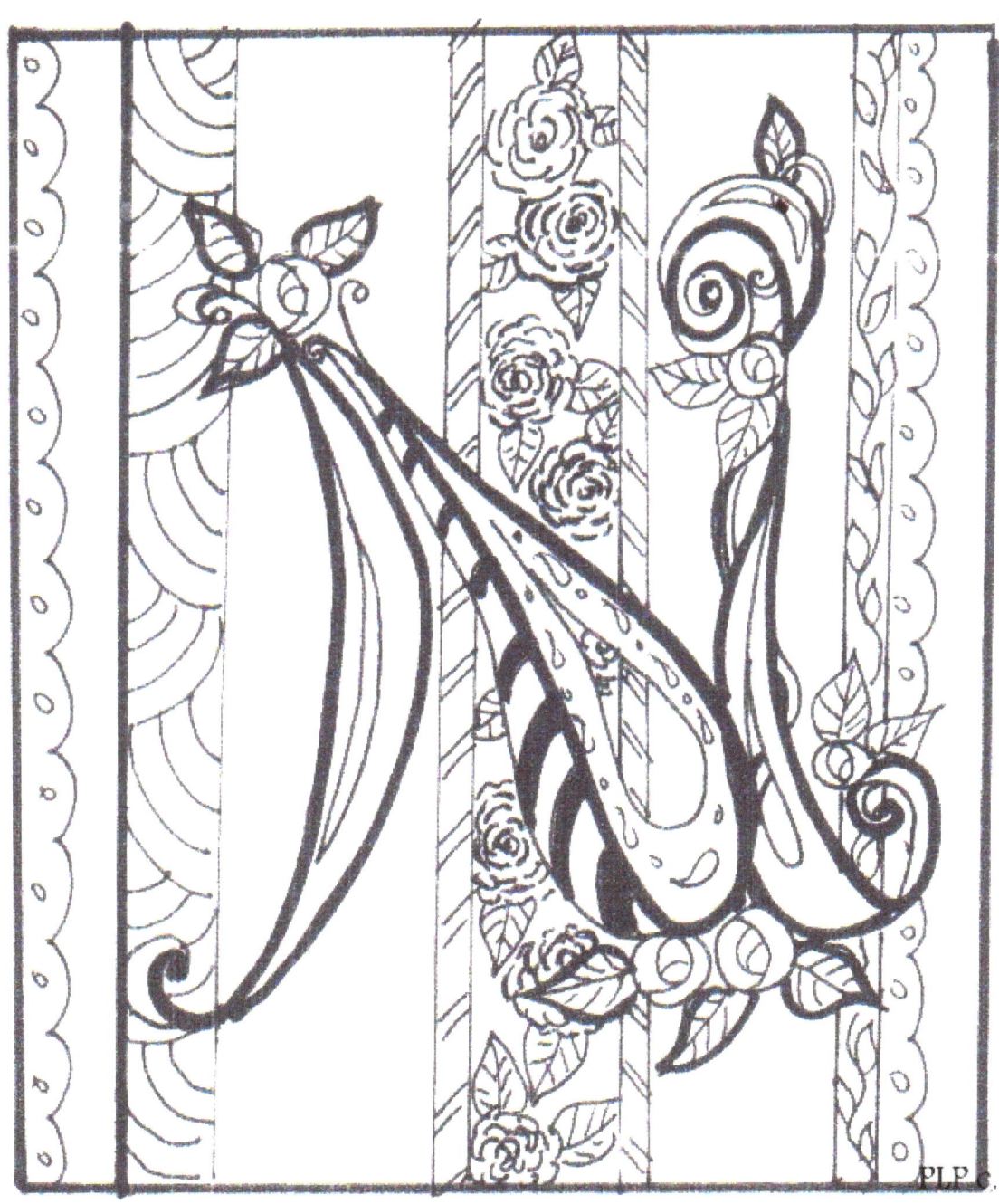

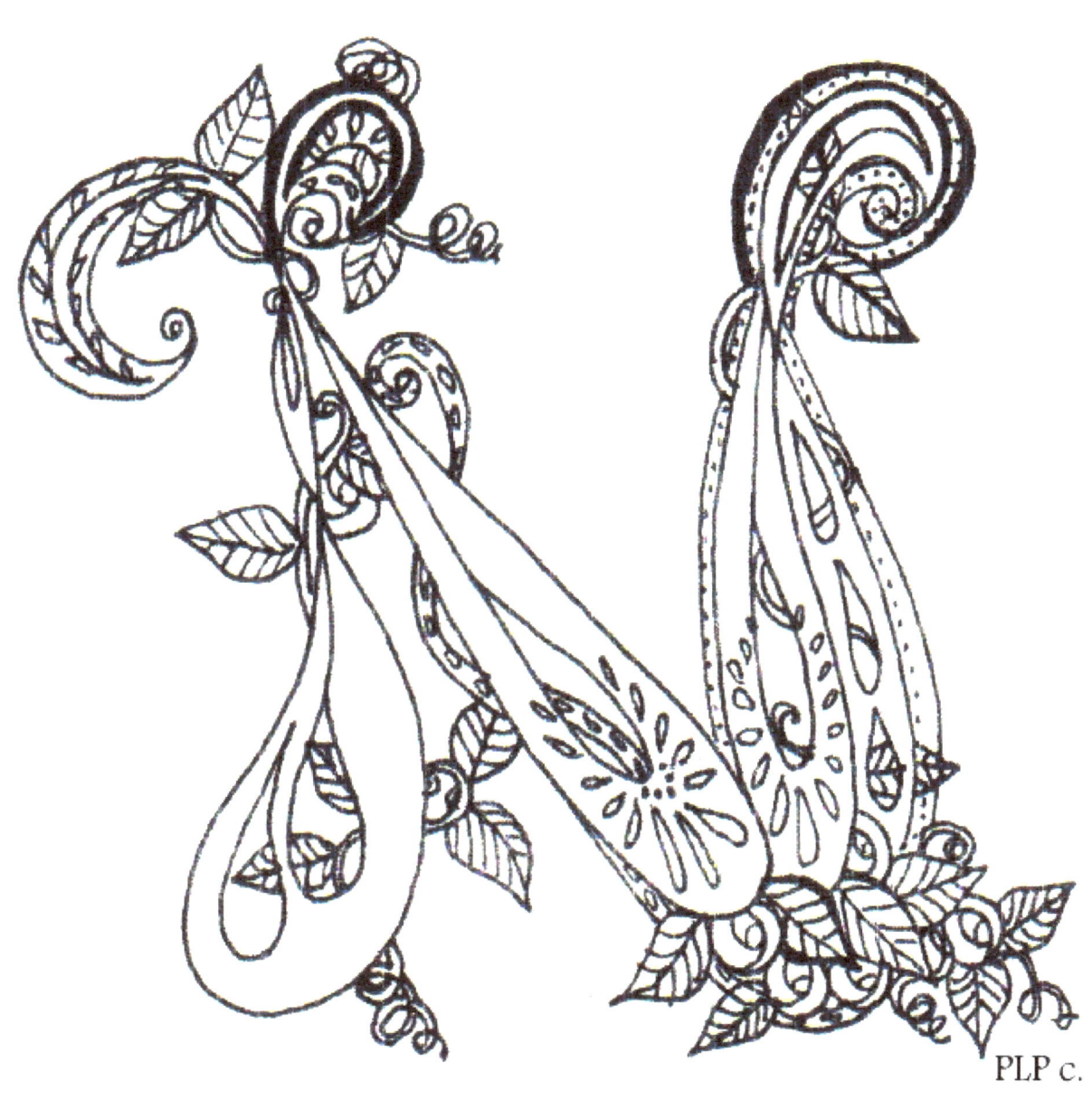

PLP c.

Just for fun try this silly N.

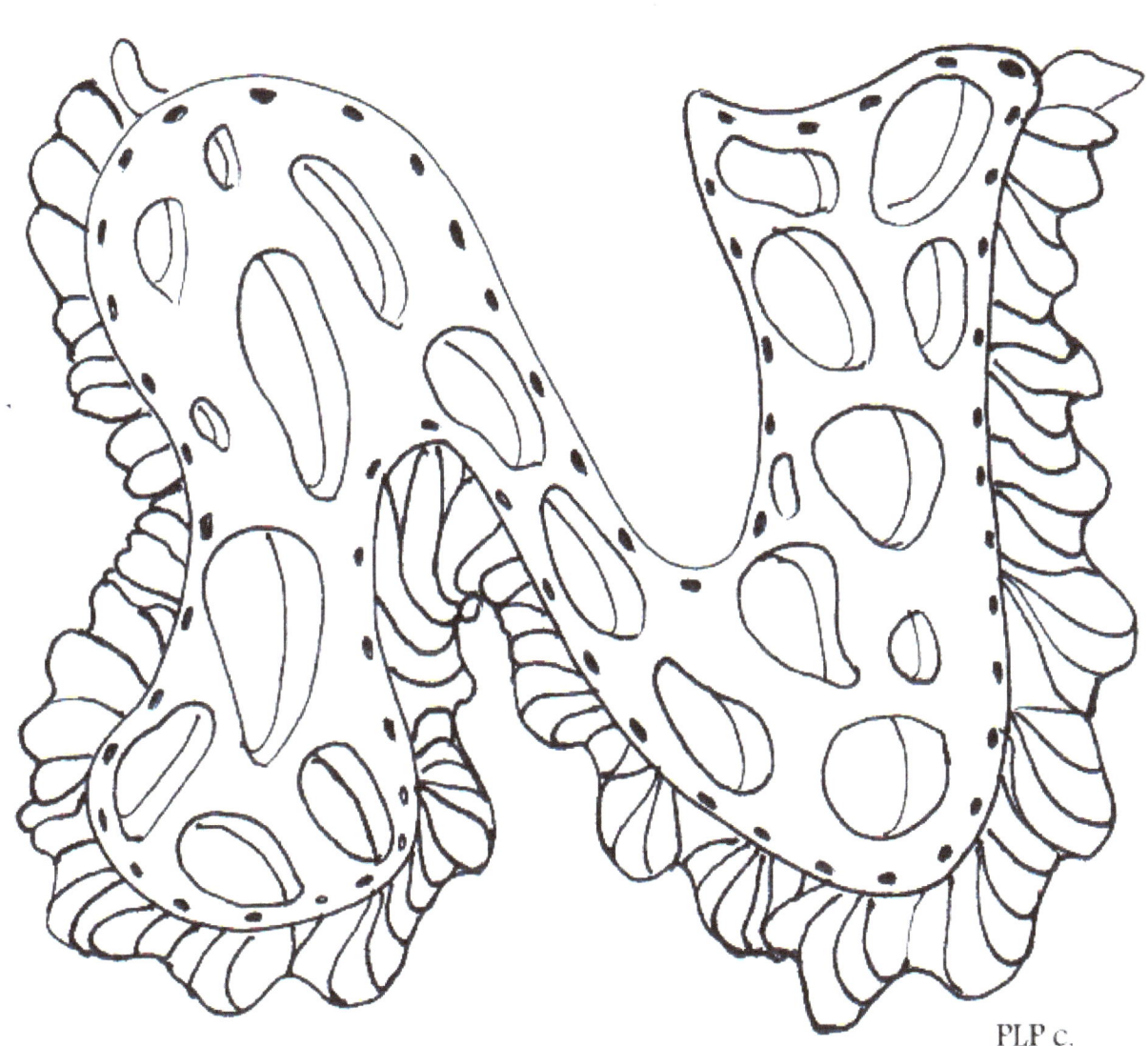

PLP c.

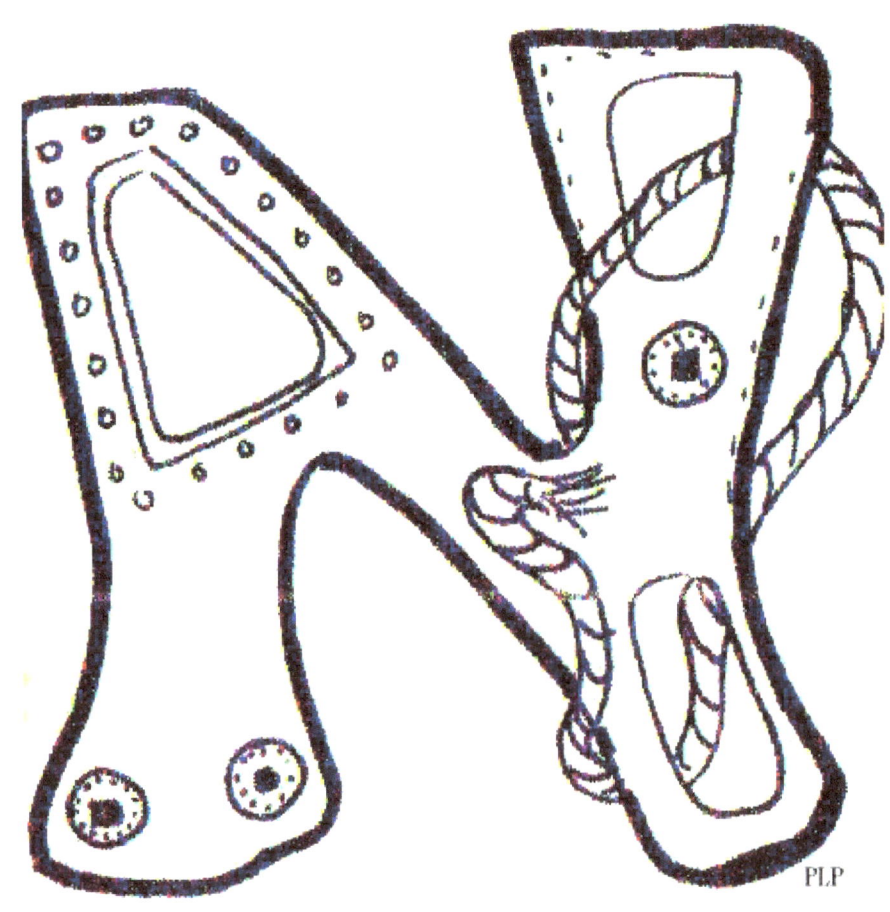

PLP

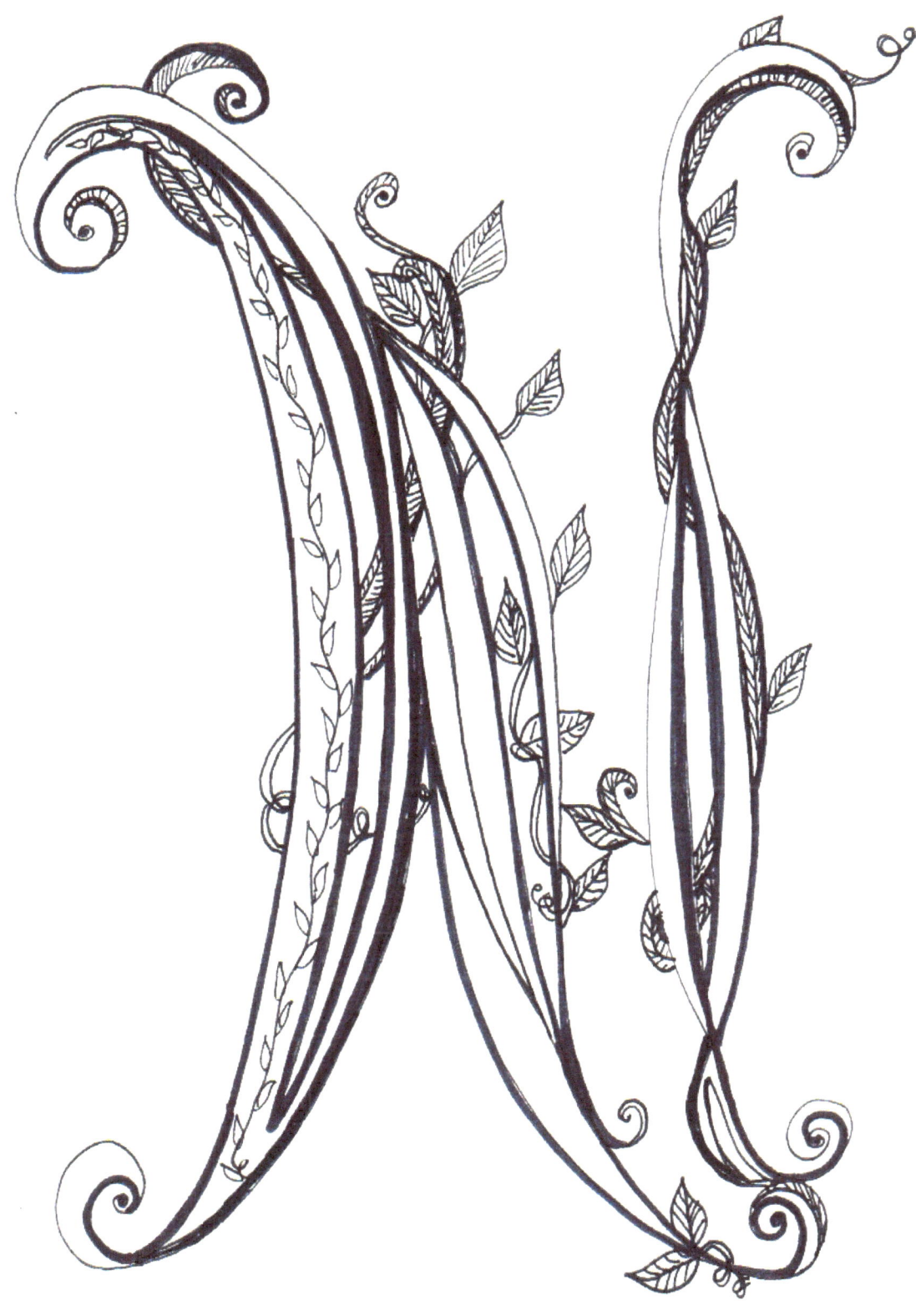

PLP
©2010

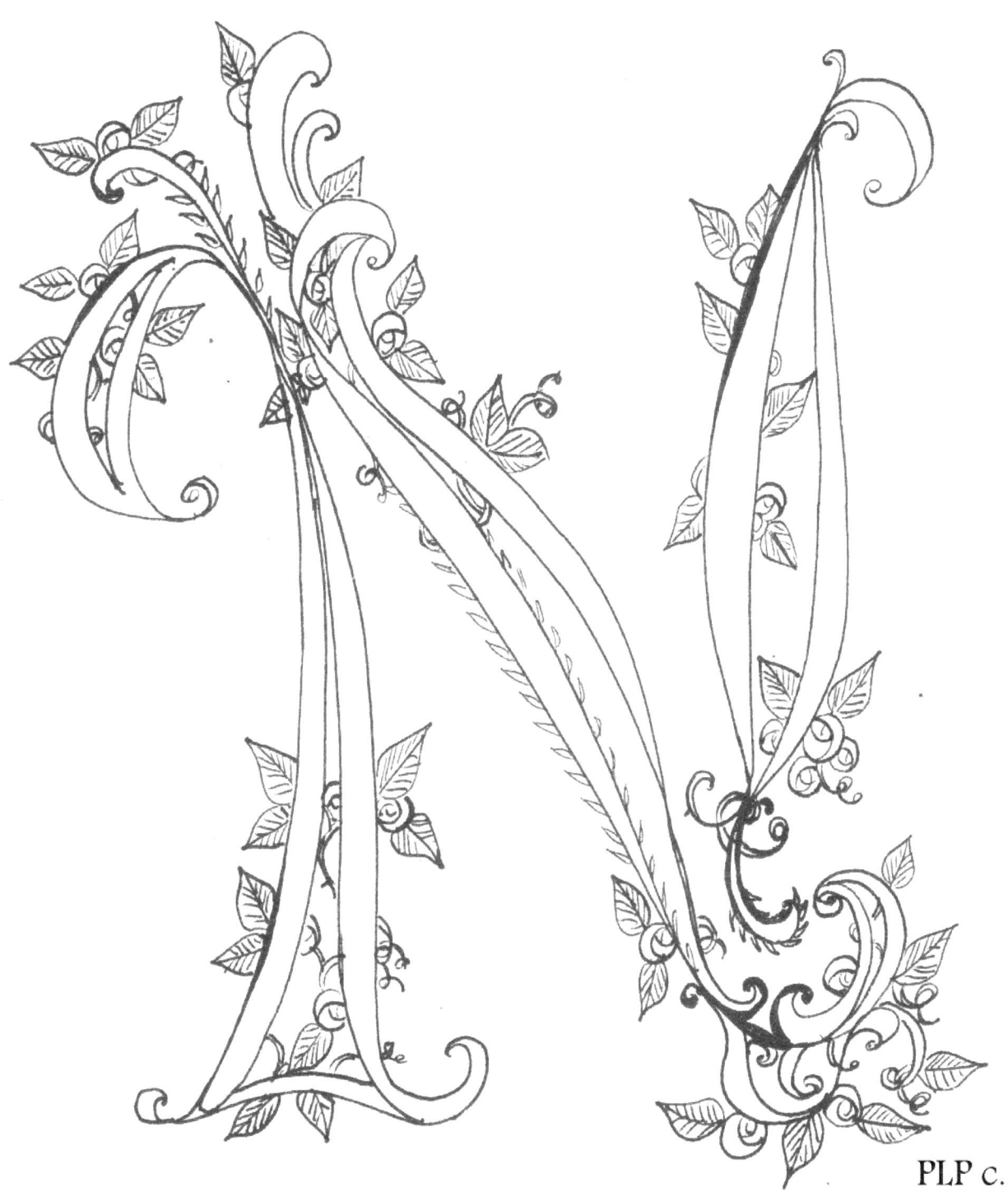

PLP c.

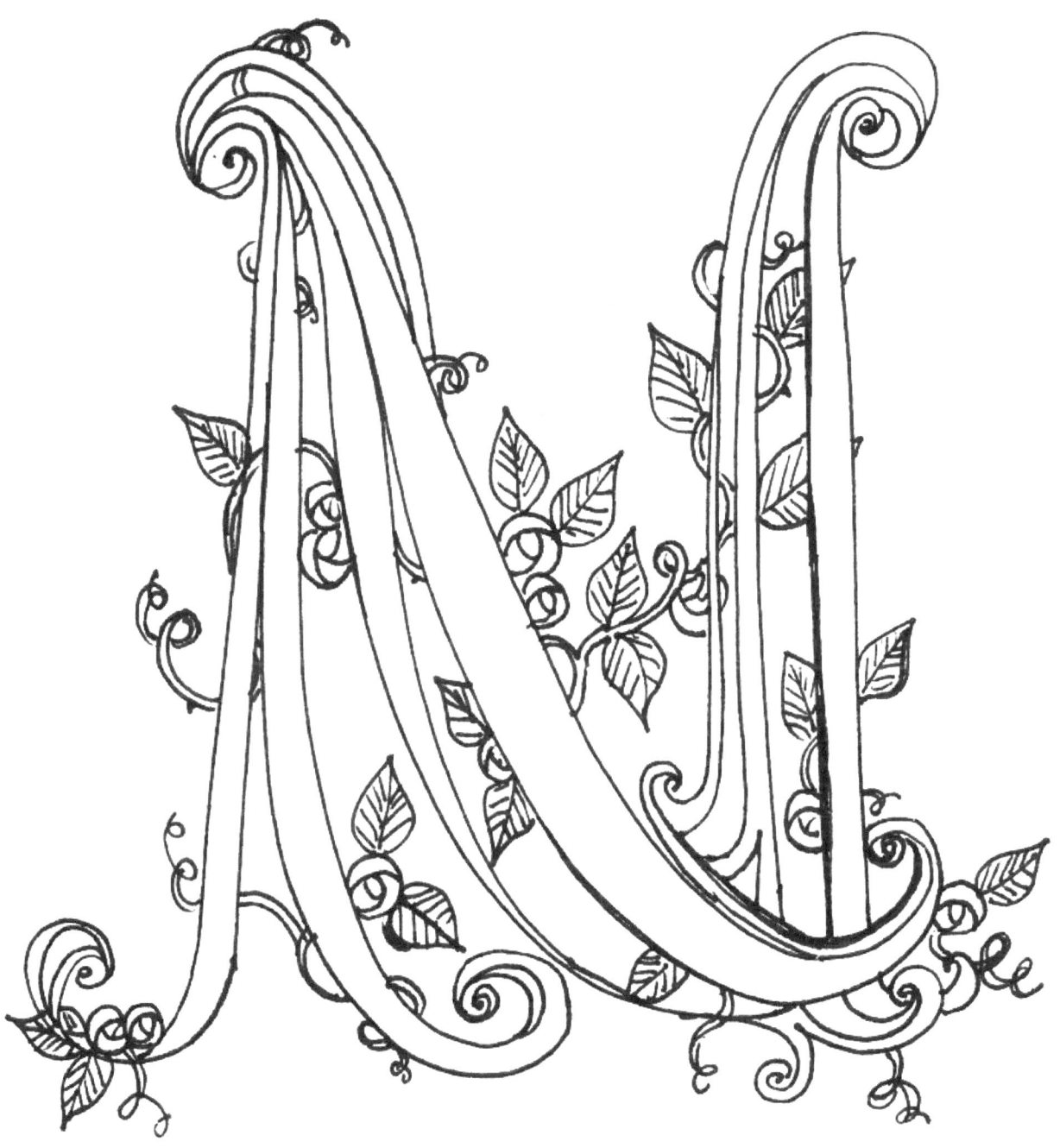

PLP c.

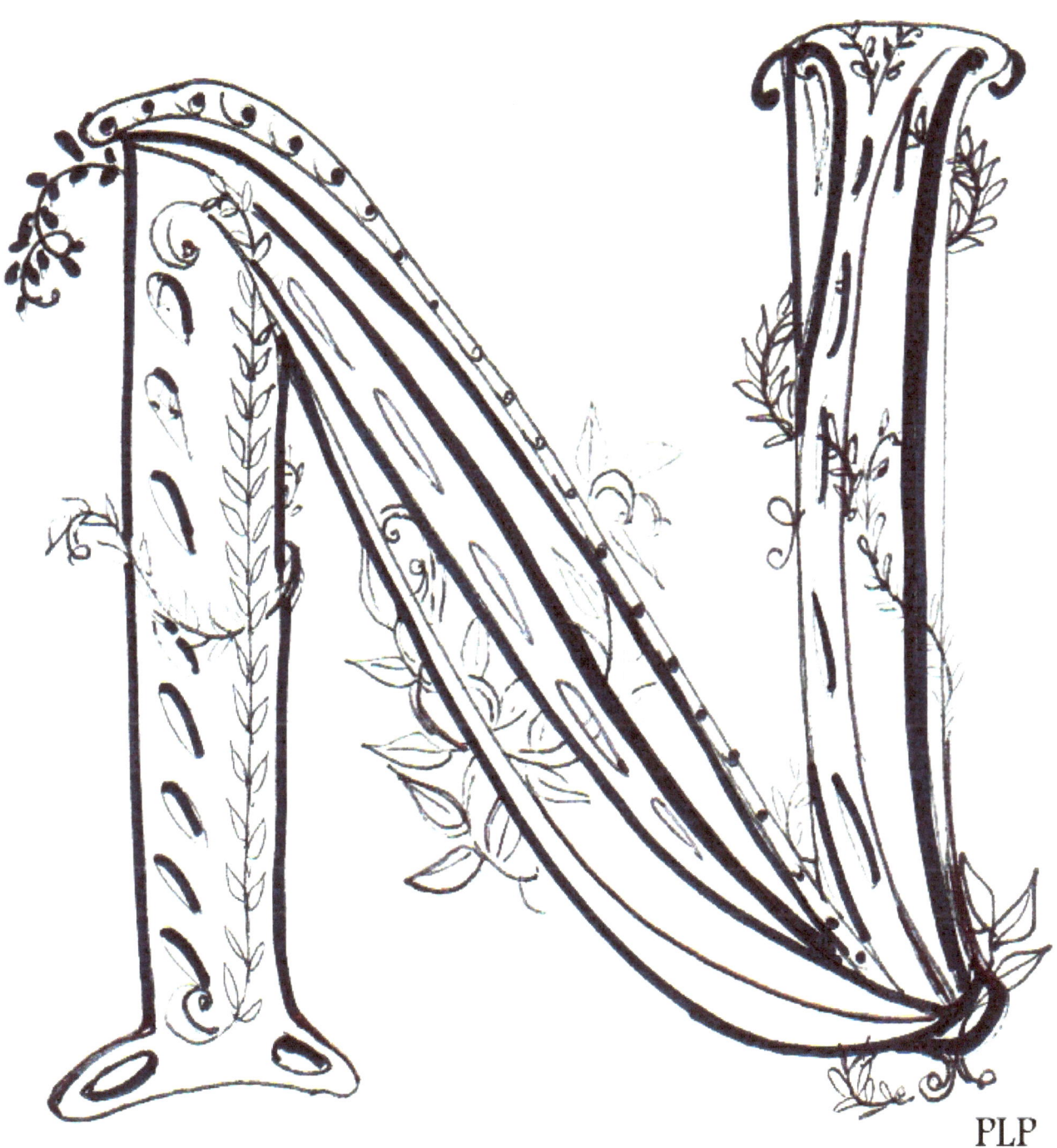

PLP

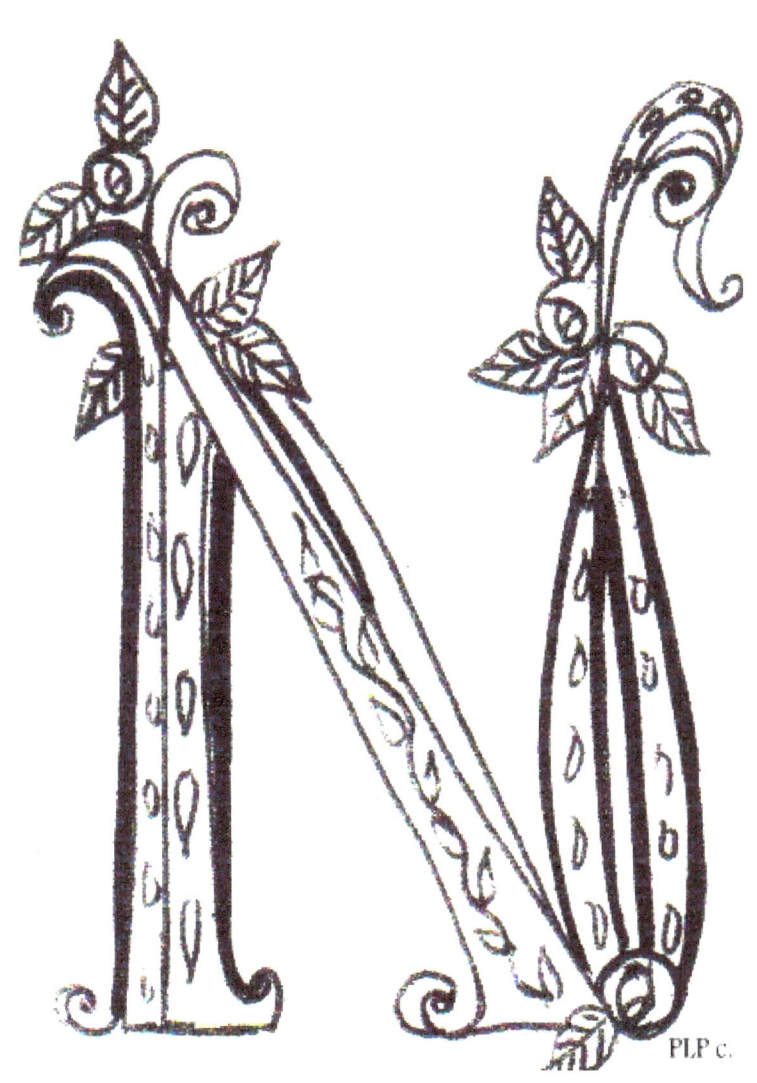

PLP c.

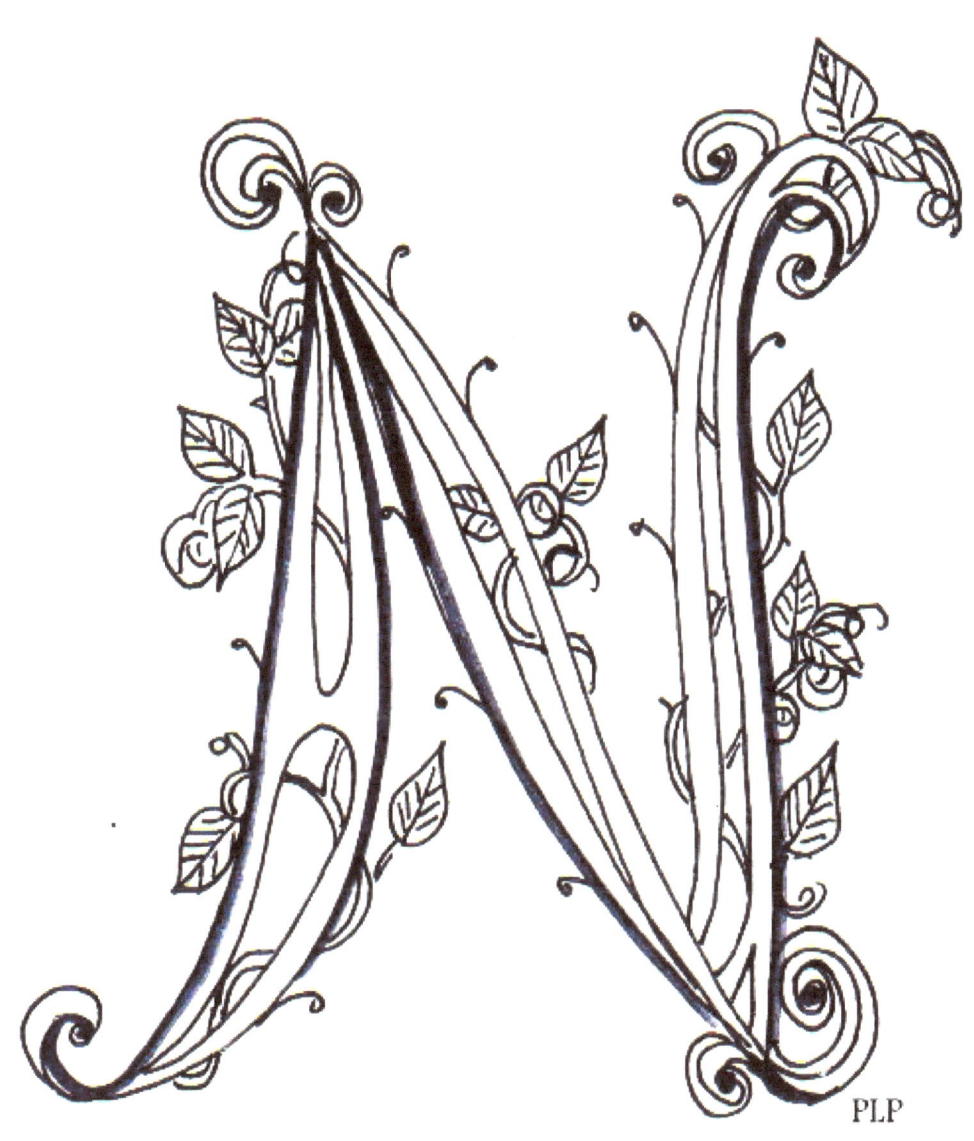

PLP

The Letter N can be filled with all kinds of design work and things found in nature. This one looks like a letter growing both designs and plants. N Letters are very fun to add things onto and into.

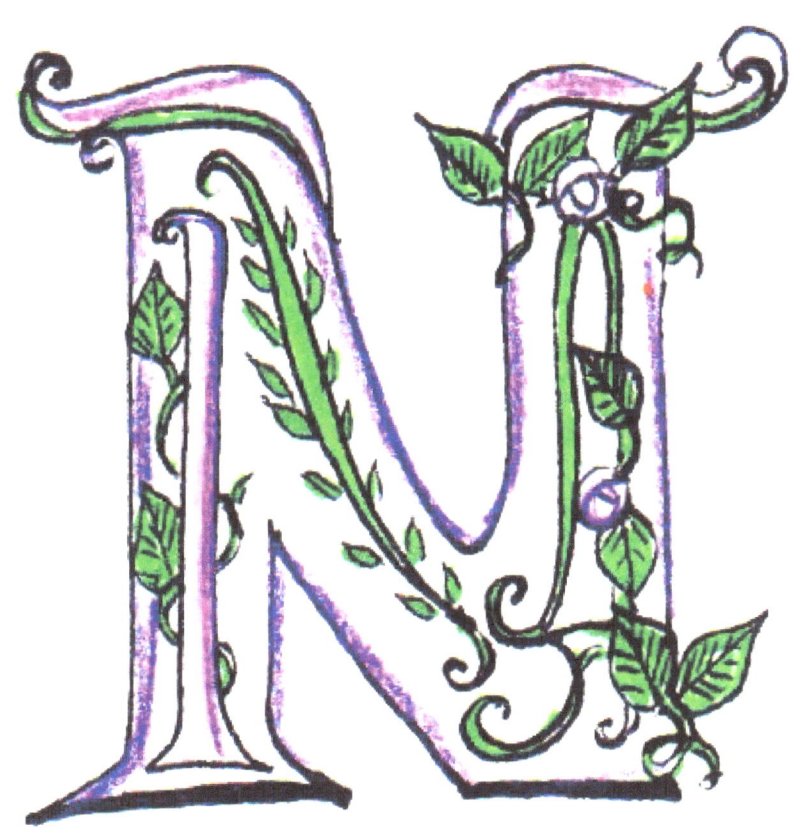

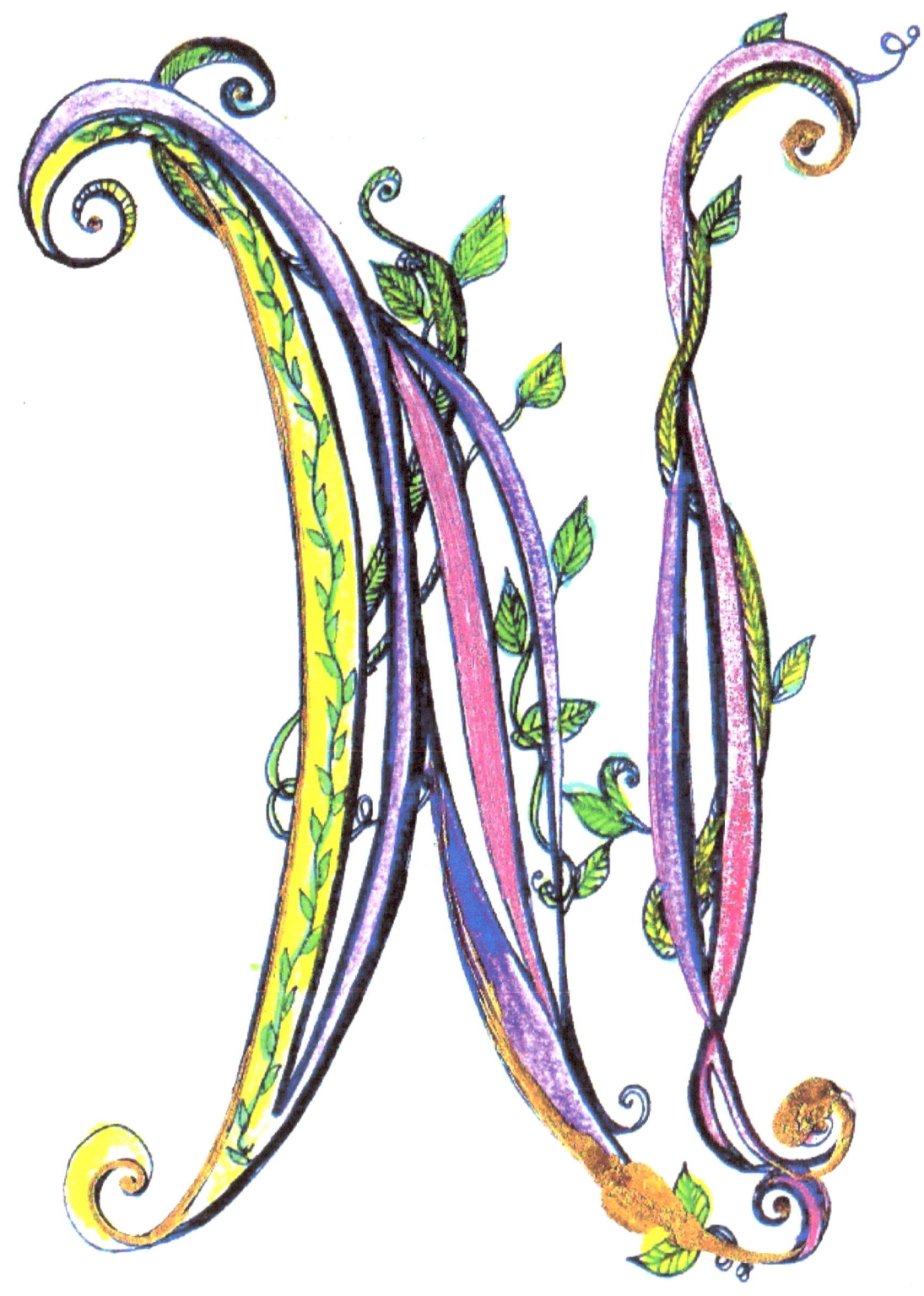

P&P
2010

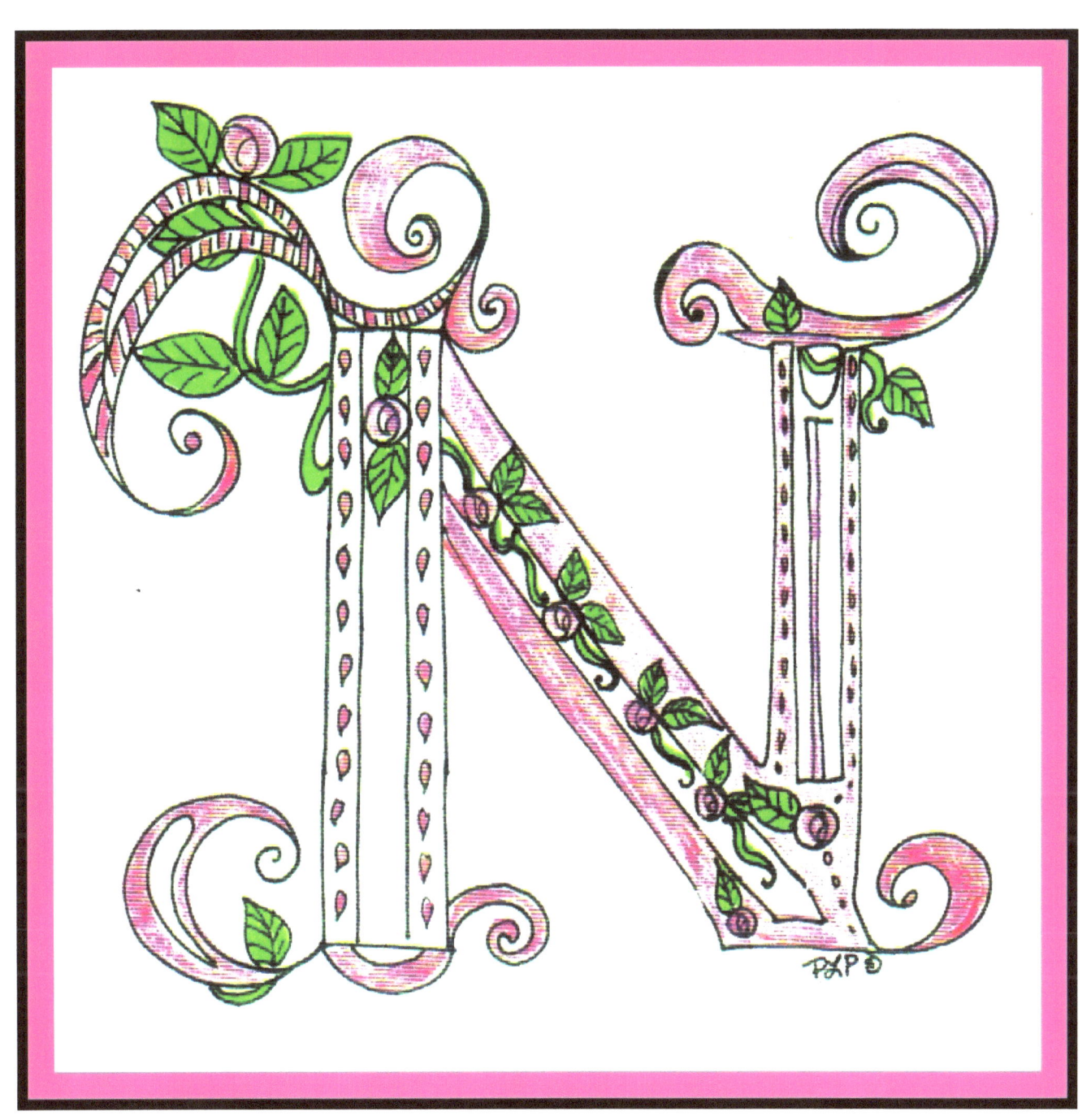

The Noble N

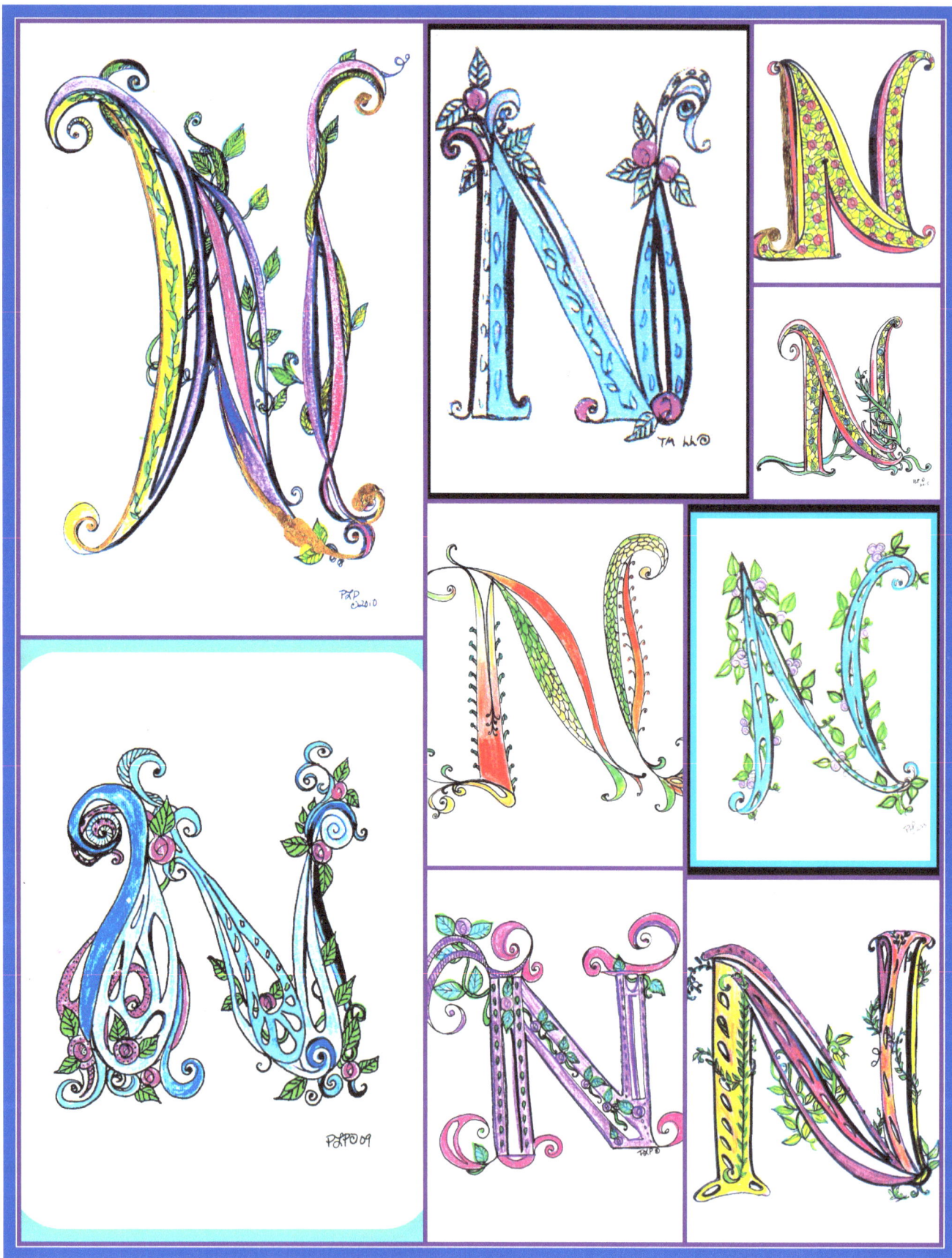

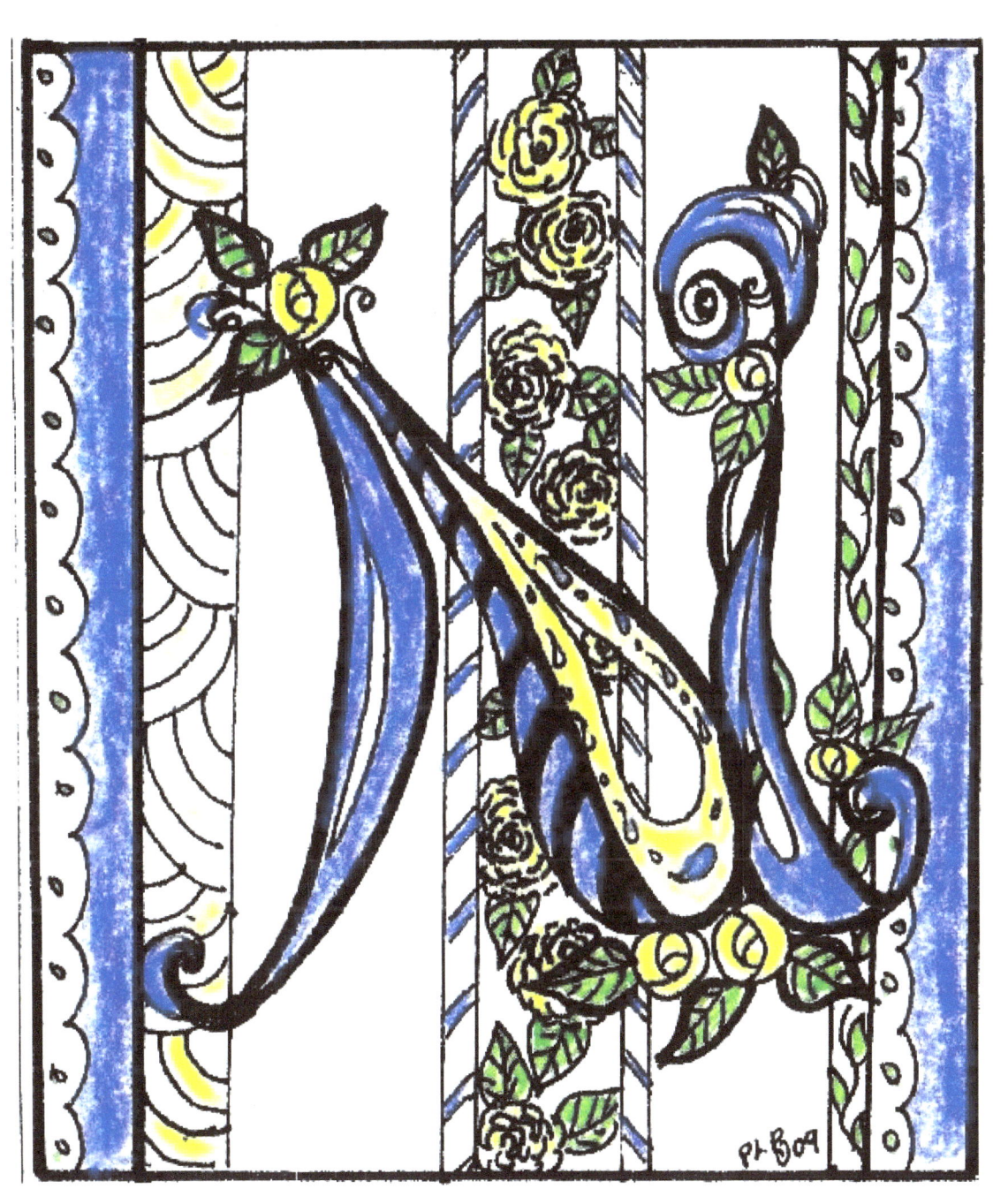

Perhaps this N was formed like wheat.

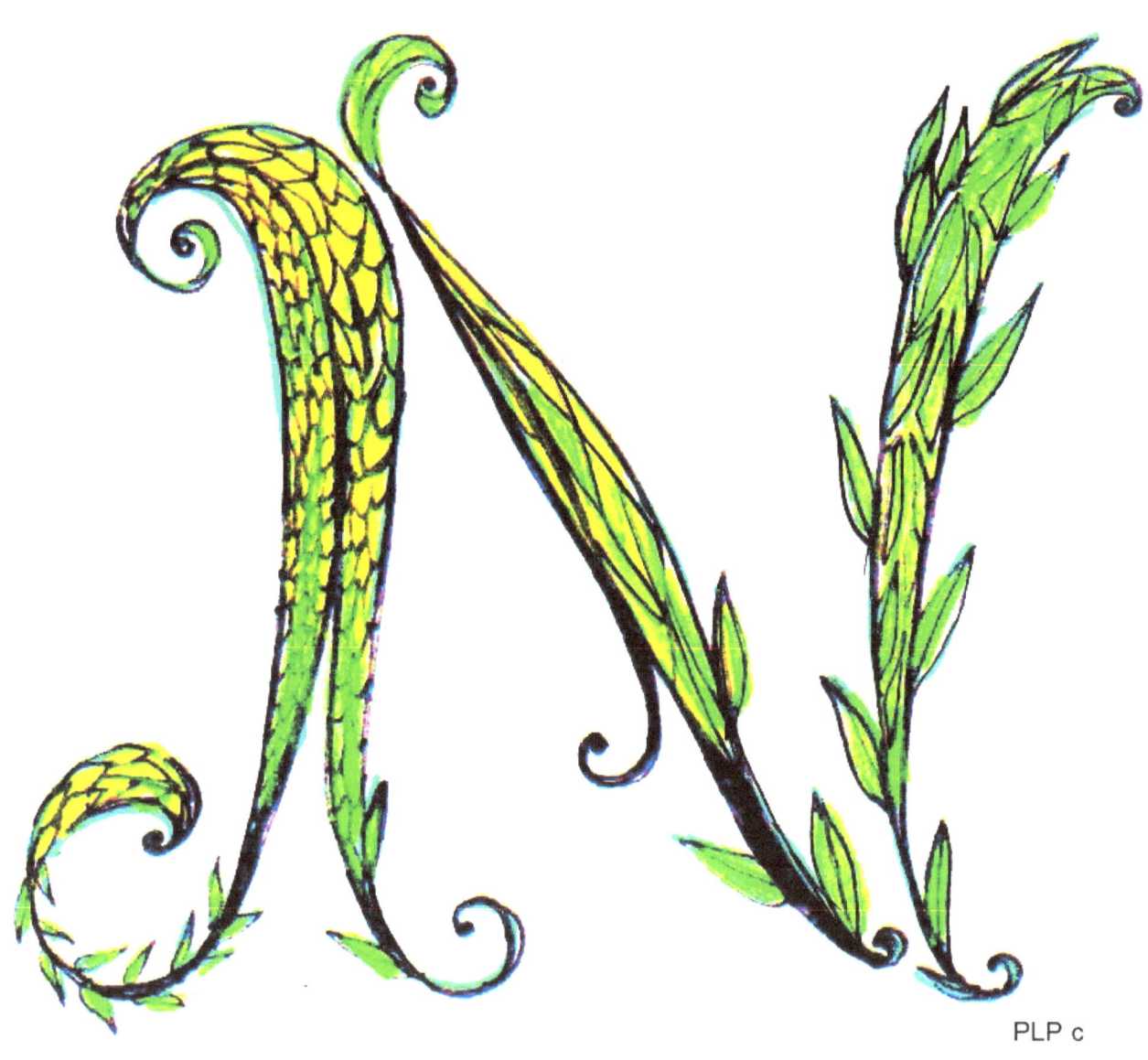

PLP c

This N looks a bit COWBOY.

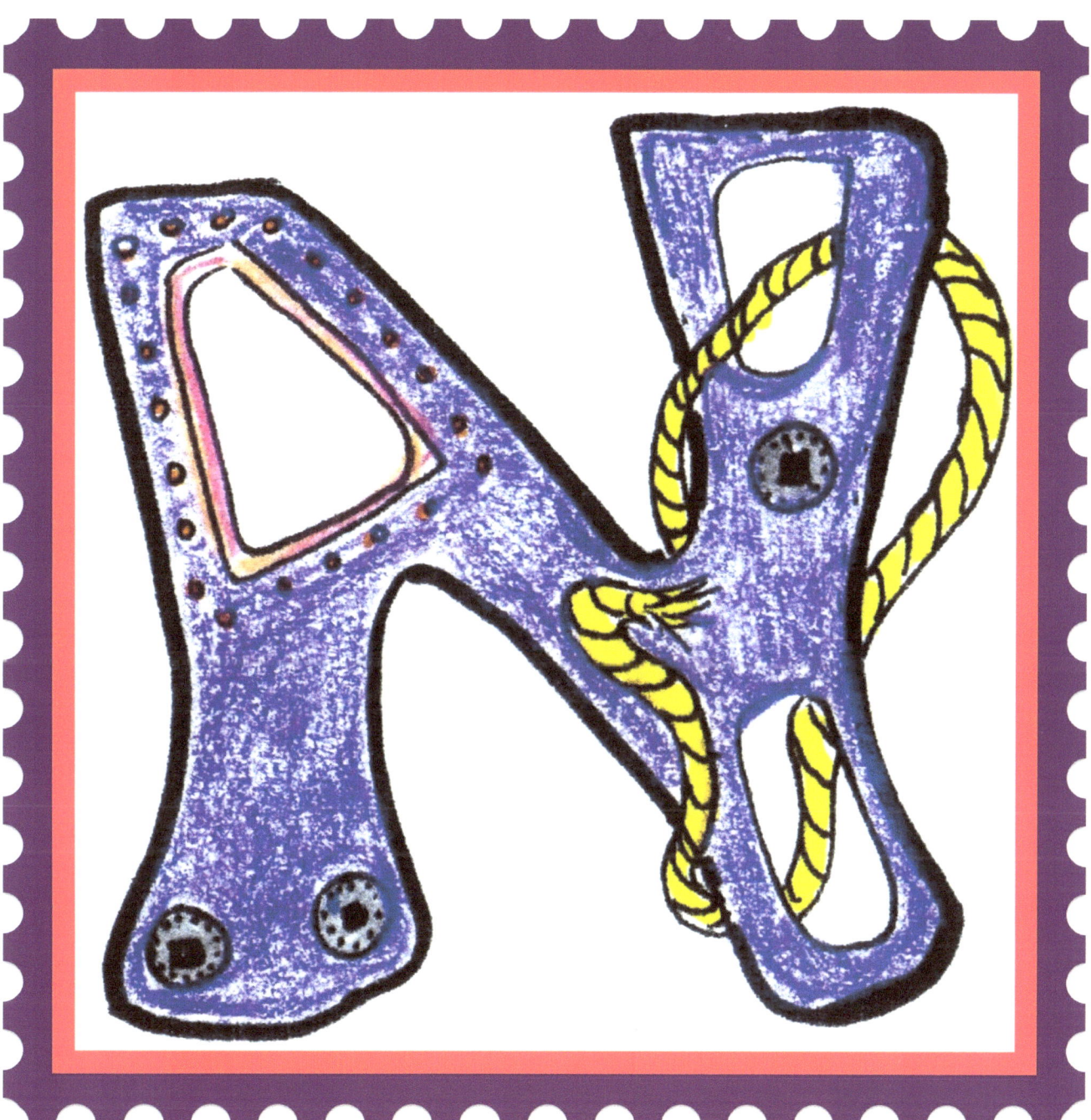

I hope you have enjoyed this coloring adventure with Noble Letter N. If you would like some more letters to try look up the other letter books of Peggy Louise Parrish.